Did you hear the one about the watering can?

> *Yeah, I almost wet my plants!*

What would you get if you crossed Garfield with a Dr. Seuss story?

> *The Fat Cat in the Hat!*

What do you call an exhausted bear?

> *Winnie the Pooped!*

Also by Jim Davis
Published by Ballantine Books:

GARFIELD'S SON OF BIG FAT HAIRY JOKES

Created by
Jim Davis

Written by
Jim Kraft and
Mark Acey

BALLANTINE BOOKS • NEW YORK

Copyright © 1994 United Feature Syndicate, Inc.

All rights reserved under International and Pan-American Copyright Conventions. Published in the United States of America by Ballantine Books, a division of Random House, Inc., New York, and simultaneously in Canada by Random House of Canada Limited, Toronto.

Library of Congress Catalog Card Number: 93-94036

ISBN 0-345-38953-0

Manufactured in the United States of America

First Edition: July 1994

10 9 8 7 6 5 4 3 2 1

CONTENTS

FAT CAT FUNNIES

What would you get if you crossed Garfield with poison ivy?
A cat who's itching to eat everything!

How does Garfield feel about winter?
It leaves him cold!

What would you get if you crossed Garfield with a rapper?
Heavy G!

What belongs to Garfield but is used more by Jon?
Garfield's name!

Why does Garfield scratch himself?
He's the only one who knows where it itches!

What is Garfield's favorite soap opera?
"One Life to Eat"

Why did Garfield stick a fish in Jon's CD player?
He wanted to listen to some sole music!

What did Garfield say when Nermal fell in the manhole?
Nothing. He was too busy laughing!

Why is Garfield fat, orange, and furry?
Because if he were skinny, white, and hairless, he'd be a clothesline!

What did the mother pig say to the little pig?
"Eat well, but don't make a Garfield of yourself!"

Did you hear about Garfield's new job?
He's a physical fatness instructor!

Why did Garfield hit Odie with a broom?
Because he couldn't find a baseball bat!

What's orange and black and has a whale of an appetite?
Moby Garfield.

Why did Garfield kick Odie off the table?
Because it was more fun than pushing him!

Does Garfield eat too much of one thing?
Garfield eats too much of everything!

What crime did Garfield commit in the bakery?
Pie-jacking!

What does Garfield call it when he eats three desserts?
Cutting back.

Why did Garfield wear running shoes to bed?
So he could fall fast asleep!

Garfield is so fat, when he gets on the scale it says, "No livestock, please!"

Garfield is so fat, when he goes in the ocean he has to watch out for harpoons!

Garfield is so fat, walking around him is an overnight trip!

Garfield is so fat, he could be the fifty-first state!

Garfield is so fat, he makes a hippo look anorexic!

Garfield is so fat, he has to wear license plates!

Garfield is so fat, Jon takes him for a roll around the block!

Garfield is so fat, he feels claustrophobic in the Astrodome!

Garfield is so fat, Goodyear wanted to fly him over the Super Bowl!

Garfield is so fat, he got thrown out of sumo wrestling for being overweight!

Garfield is so fat, he shouldn't be on a leash—he should be tied up to a dock!

Garfield is so fat, his tummy and his tail are in different time zones!

Garfield got rid of his alarm clock. Do you know how he woke up?
Happier!

Will Garfield ever run for president?
The only thing Garfield will ever run for is lunch!

How is Garfield like a race-car driver?
He spends a lot of time on laps!

How did Garfield get rid of the dalmatian?
He used spot remover!

Why does Garfield walk on two legs?
Because Jon refuses to carry him!

They say that Garfield sleeps like a log. But the log is easier to wake up!

How is Garfield like Jon's doctor?
They both give Jon lots of shots!

Jon: "What should I serve with my meat loaf?"
Garfield: "The antidote."

Jon: "Garfield, do you know what to do if the house catches on fire?"

Garfield: "Why? Are you fixing the toaster again?"

Jon: "Garfield, why did you put Nermal in the garbage can?"

Garfield: "Because he's too big to flush!"

What did Garfield say to the ghost?

"Why don't you get real?"

What's the difference between Garfield and a great white shark?

One is a ferocious eater and the other is a fish.

What would you get if you crossed Garfield with a polar bear?

One thing's for sure—you'd never get it out of the fridge!

What goes up but never comes down?

Garfield's opinion of himself!

DID YOU HEAR THE ONE ABOUT...?

(It's a big joke!)

Did you hear the one about Odie?
It's a no-brainer!

Did you hear the one about the toothache?
It's a pain!

Did you hear the one about the electric eel?
It's shocking!

Did you hear the one about the lasagna?
It was panned!

Did you hear the one about Garfield's tummy?
It's a big waist!

Did you hear the one about the tornado?
It'll blow you away!

Did you hear the one about the dynamite?
It's a blast!

Did you hear the one about the frog?
It's toadly hilarious!

Did you hear the one about the snake?
It's hiss-terical!

Did you hear the one about the asteroid?
It's out-of-this-world!

Did you hear the one about the chili?
It's hot stuff!

Did you hear the one about Odie's tongue?
It's a mouthful!

Did you hear the one about the elevator?
It has its ups and downs!

Did you hear the one about Garfield's burp?
It brought down the house!

Did you hear the one about the owl?
It's a hoot!

Did you hear the one about the boxer?
It'll knock you out!

Did you hear the one about the jungle?
It's wild!

Did you hear the one about Pooky?
It's a bear!

Did you hear the one about the helium balloon?
It's a gas!

Did you hear the one about Jon's cooking?
It's too hard to swallow!

Did you hear the one about the new pencil?
It's pointless!

Did you hear the one about the sky?
It's over your head!

Did you hear the one about the diamond?
It's a real gem!

Did you hear the one about the floor?
It's beneath you!

Did you hear the one about the drill?
It's boring!

Did you hear the one about the skunk?
It stinks!

Did you hear the one about the chicken?
It's really fowl!

Did you hear the one about the cookie?
It's crumby!

Did you hear the one about the air conditioner?
It's so cool!

Did you hear the one about Garfield's alarm clock?
It's a smash!

Did you hear the one about the ocean?
It's all wet!

Did you hear the one about the donkey?
It's asinine!

Did you hear the one about the vacuum cleaner?
It sucks!

Did you hear the one about the garbage truck?
It's picking up!

Did you hear the one about the bowling ball?
It's right up your alley!

Did you hear the one about the surgeon?
It'll leave you in stitches!

Did you hear the one about the canyon?
It's grand!

Did you hear the one about the coal mine?
It's pretty deep!

Did you hear the one about the phone?
It has a familiar ring!

Did you hear the one about the desert?
It's pretty dry!

Did you hear the one about the boomerang?
It'll come back to you!

Did you hear the one about the wheel?
It's going around!

Did you hear the one about amnesia?
It's easy to forget!

Did you hear the one about the redwood?
It's tree-mendous!

Did you hear the one about the rocket?
It's gonna go far!

Did you hear the one about the *Titanic*?
It'll give you a sinking feeling!

Did you hear the one about the terrible twins?
It's two bad!

What would you get if you crossed a vegetable with a famous talk-show host?
Okra Winfrey!

What's yellow, shapely, and turns letters on "Wheel of Fortune"?
Banana White!

What would you get if you crossed a famous children's book author with a Greek god?
Dr. Zeus!

What would you get if you crossed Garfield with a famous pop singer?
Belly Joel!

What has four legs, a curly tail, and an IQ of 200?
Albert Einswine!

What would you get if you crossed a supermodel with
a crayfish?
Cindy Crawdad!

What soul-singing vegetable used to be married to
Ike?
Tina Turnip!

Who is Odie's favorite rapper?
Barky Bark!

What would you get if you crossed a TV commentator
with a cheese?
Rush Limburger!

What would you get if you crossed a famous basketball
coach with a bad dream?
Bobby Knightmare!

What would you get if you crossed a fruit with a female pop star?
Papaya Carey!

What vegetable was known as "The King of Rock 'n' Roll"?
Elvis Parsley!

What would you get if you crossed a famous horror writer with a movie ape?
Stephen Kong!

What would you get if you crossed Prince Charles with Moby Dick?
The Prince of Whales!

What would you get if you crossed an Oscar-winning actress with Jon's cooking?
Katharine Heartburn!

What singing vegetable was "Grown in the USA"?
Bruce Stringbean!

What's yellow, fuzzy, and too tired to eat honey?
Winnie the Pooped!

What would you get if you crossed Odie with a ghost-chasing cartoon dog?
Scooby Doofus!

What would you get if you crossed Garfield with a Muppet?
Kermit the Hog!

What would you get if you crossed Garfield with a green superhero?
The Incredible Bulk!

What happened to Rin Tin Tin after he went on a diet?
He became Thin Tin Tin!

What would you get if you crossed a nearsighted cartoon geezer with a peanut?
Mr. Magoober!

24

What would you get if you crossed Odie with a cartoon sailor?
Pupeye!

What Steven Spielberg smash featured huge, prehistoric dogs?
Jurassic Bark!

What would you get if you crossed Garfield with John Travolta?
Saturday Night Feline!

What would you get if you crossed Jon with a famous movie about UFOs?
Close Encounters of the Nerd Kind!

What would you call a leopard that never takes a bath?
The Stink Panther!

What would you get if you crossed Garfield with a famous Shakespeare play?
Romeow and Juliet!

What would you get if you crossed Odie with a late-
    night talk-show host?
Arsenio Howl!

What would you get if you crossed Odie with a well-
    known actress?
Droolia Roberts!

Who is Odie's favorite country singer?
Arf Brooks!

What would you get if you crossed Garfield with a
    Tom Cruise movie?
Top Gut!

What would you get if you crossed a vegetable with
    baseball's all-time hit king?
Beet Rose!

Did you hear about the famous Russian dancer who
    was under the weather?
He had a Baryshnicough!

What would you get if you crossed the star of *City Slickers* with an ornate ceiling fixture?
Billy Crystal Chandelier!

What would you get if you crossed Superman with an avid sunbather?
The Tan of Steel!

What had four legs, a curly tail, and artistic genius?
Pablo Pigasso!

What is Odie's favorite Sylvester Stallone movie?
Rambone.

What has one ear, carries a paint brush, and can walk through walls?
Vincent van Ghost!

What famous starship captain has some odd habits?
Captain James T. Quirk!

27

What cowboy hero fought crabgrass throughout the
    West?
The Lawn Ranger!

What famous horror film featured ghostly chickens?
Poultrygeist!

What would you get if you crossed Garfield with the
    Caped Crusader?
Fatman!

What has four legs, two Oscars, and no brains?
Odie Foster!

JOCK TALK

Did you hear about the dinosaur who plays football for Denver?
He's a Broncosaurus!

What football game should dieters avoid?
The Sugar Bowl!

What did the soccer ball say to the soccer player?
"I get a kick out of you!"

What is half man, half horse, and catches flies?
A centaurfielder!

Garfield will never be a good basketball player. He shoots too many hair balls!

Can Jon catch a football?
He can't even catch his breath!

Why was the batter swinging a broom?
He was the clean-up hitter!

Who is Garfield's favorite NBA star?
Shaquille O'Meal!

Which athletes are the worst people?
Tennis players. They have a lot of faults!

What's the difference between Odie and a football?
Garfield doesn't enjoy kicking a football.

"Why is this batter hitting so many foul balls?"
"Maybe he's in a foul mood!"

When is a football player like Garfield after dinner?
When's he's a *full*back!

What did the dartboard say to the dart?
"I get your point."

What would you get if you crossed Odie with a famous
    college football team?
Notre Dumb!

What is Garfield's favorite type of ball?
A meatball!

What's the difference between a dog and a hockey
    puck?
About 2 IQ points.

What is the only baseball position Garfield can play?
Designated sitter!

Which athletes are the angriest?
Golfers. They're always teed off!

What kind of dog spends all New Year's Day watching
    football?
A bowl dog!

What do cheerleaders drink during a game?
Root beer!

Which sport is the most romantic?
Tennis. There's "love" in every game!

What's the difference between a football center and
Garfield?
One's a big snapper and the other's a big napper!

Who is Odie's favorite NBA star?
Scottie Puppen!

What is the first thing Jon does after he putts?
Replaces the divot.

What would you get if you crossed a basketball player
with a large, aquatic mammal?
A hoopopotamus!

What's the difference between Nermal and a football?
A football doesn't whine when you spike it!

What do you call a golf ball hit by Jon?
Lost.

Who is Garfield's all-time favorite catcher?
Johnny Brunch!

Why did the hockey player color his teeth orange?
So they'd be easier to find on the ice.

How is Jon like a professional golfer?
He gets lots of advice from his catty!

What would you get if you crossed a Hall of Fame running back with a biblical strongman?
O. J. Samson!

What would you get if you crossed Jon with a famous home-run hitter?
Boob Ruth!

What NFL team should Jon play for?
The Cincinnati Bungles!

What kind of athletic shoes do monkeys wear?
Treeboks!

Golfer 1: "This golf course must have lots of sand
     traps."
Golfer 2: "What makes you say that?"
Golfer 1: "They just loaded our clubs on a camel!"

Which NFL team would you not entrust with your val-
     uables?
The Pittsburgh Stealers!

What kind of dog can catch a football?
A wide retriever!

What did the golf ball say to the golf club?
"You drive me wild!"

What's the difference between Ozzie Smith and Odie?
One's a great shortstop and the other's a great door-
     stop!

What would you get if you crossed a hockey player
    with a comic actress?
Goalie Hawn!

Garfield: "Jon's like lightning on skis."
Nermal: "He goes really fast, huh?"
Garfield: "No, he's always hitting trees!"

Garfield: "I spent all morning practicing archery with
    Odie."
Nermal: "How did it go?"
Garfield: "Not so good. I only hit him once."

Jon: "Garfield, you need to learn more about baseball.
    Do you know what RBI stands for?"
Garfield: "Really Boring Information."

What would you get if you crossed Evander Holyfield
    with Jon?
The heavyweight chump!

What former NBA star goes great with coffee?
Cream Abdul-Jabbar!

When is a baseball like a bad kid?
When it's grounded!

ALL THE JOKES YOU CAN EAT!

What kind of food improves your vision?
See-food!

What would you get if you mixed pasta with bugs?
Vermincelli!

What is Garfield's least favorite pasta dish?
Spaghetti and mothballs!

What do you call a lizard who's a vegetarian?
A saladmander!

What's round, chocolatey, and swings through the
trees?
A chocolate chimp cookie!

What is Garfield's favorite kind of tree?
Poultry!

Why was the butcher fired?
He was always making misteaks!

Where does Queen Elizabeth shop for her dinner?
Get real! She makes her servants do it for her.

What do you call a Chinese dish that's been in the
fridge for a month?
Egg Foo Old!

Kid 1: "Adam and Eve must have been pretty fat."
Kid 2: "Why do you say that?"
Kid 1: " 'Cause they lived in the garden of Eatin'!"

What is Jacques Cousteau's favorite sandwich?
Peanut butter and jellyfish!

Why did the baker quit making doughnuts?
He was sick of the hole business!

Knock, knock!
Who's there?
Dewey.
Dewey who?
Dewey you-ey like chop suey?

Why did the man wear banana peels on his feet?
Because they make great slippers!

When is a cannibal like an aardvark?
When he's an aunt-eater!

What did the cannibal say to the explorer?
"Pleased to eat you."

How does Garfield eat a big meal?
One shovelful at a time!

What's huge and sweet and full of sand?
The Sahara Dessert!

What is Jon's favorite food?
Anything Garfield doesn't steal from him!

What is Odie's favorite dessert?
Pooch cobbler!

What's the difference between Garfield and butter?
Garfield has more fat!

What did the gravy say to the mashed potatoes?
"I've got you covered."

Why did Odie bring scissors to the dinner table?
Because Jon said he should try to cut calories.

What dessert is always served in heaven?
Angel food cake!

Why did the dumb chef put a hen in his cake batter?
He was trying to make a layer cake!

What did the vegetables say to the stew meat?
"We're all going to pot!"

What would you get if you crossed Jon with a dessert
    topping?
Wimped cream!

What would you get if you mixed Jon with a can of
    beans?
Dork and beans!

What would you get if you mixed a hummingbird with
    ground beef?
A humburger!

Jon and Garfield went into a restaurant and sat down.
When the waitress arrived, Jon asked, "Do you serve
cats here?" "No," she replied, "you'll have to order
something else."

Where do pigs like to go for dinner?
To a Swinese restaurant!

Did you hear about the vegetable-powered car?
It runs on aspara-gas!

What would you get if you crossed a vegetable with Jon's former roommate?
Lyman beans!

How is a baker like a bad basketball player?
They both make turnovers!

What food comes from phantom cows?
Ghost beef!

What would you get if you mixed "Garfield and Friends" with mayonnaise and relish?
Toona salad!

What would you get if you crossed a lousy comedian with a hen?
A lot of bad yolks!

Knock, knock!
Who's there?
Marsha.
Marsha who?
Marsha-mallows! Get ready to roast!

What kind of potatoes do dogsled drivers like?
Mushed potatoes!

What is Garfield's least favorite dessert?
Lice cream!

What is Santa's favorite Easter candy?
Jolly beans!

What kind of nuts does Garfield love?
Dough-nuts!

How does a pilot cook his meals?
In a flying pan!

What dried fruit once lived in the White House?
Ronald Raisin!

Why were Garfield's sheets covered with feathers?
He'd been eating quackers in bed!

Why did the boy hold his report card over his head?
He was trying to raise his grades.

What is a little snake's favorite subject?
Hiss-tory.

When is a baseball slugger like a student?
When he does his homerwork!

"Janey, why did you skip class yesterday?"
"I had to, Mrs. Shlunk. I was suffering from illness
    and fatigue."
"Were you really?"
"Yes, I was sick and tired of school!"

Teacher: "Your grammar is very shaky."
Student: "Yes, and my grampa's not too steady either!"

How would Odie get to school?
He'd have to ride the drool bus!

Why did the little hummingbird have to stay after
school?
He didn't do his humwork!

What grade is Garfield in?
The furrest grade!

"Jason, what do two and two make?"
"Two and two are five."
"That is incorrect."
"Okay. Two and two *is* five."

"Son, would you like some help with your math homework?"
"Thanks, Dad, but I'd rather get the right answers."

What is Garfield's favorite kind of test?
A taste test!

Did you hear about the student who spent all her time at the mall?
She was majoring in buy-ology!

Why did Garfield put a tack on the teacher's chair?
He wanted to be the teacher's pest!

What would you call a surprise test about Odie?
A pup quiz!

How is a good student like a football quarterback?
They both know how to pass!

Teacher: "If I had eight pieces of candy, and I gave seven to my friend, what would I have?
Student: "You'd have a very happy friend!"

Teacher: "Why do cows eat green grass?"
Student: "Because they can't wait for it to get ripe!"

Teacher: "Why did Paul Revere take a midnight ride?"
Student: "Because he missed the 10:30 bus."

Teacher: "How many sides does a triangle have?"
Student: "Two. An inside and an outside!"

Mom: "What did you study in school today?"
Son: "Wrong division."
Mom: "I think you mean *long* division."
Son: "Not the way *I* do it!"

Principal: "Why did Mr. Glubber send you to me?"
Student: "I wiped my nose."
Principal: "What's wrong with that?"
Student: "I wiped it on his tie."

Teacher: "What is a fraction?"
Student: "I think it's the past tense of friction."

Teacher: "Jason, do you know Lincoln's 'Gettysburg
    Address'?"
Jason: "No, but give me a phone book and I'll look it
    up."

Why did the sheep flunk out of school?
He was woolly stupid!

What would you get if you crossed a snake with an
    average student?
A "C" serpent!

Why was the shark so smart?
He just ate a school of fish!

What kind of schools do eagles attend?
High schools!

What is a little wizard's favorite subject?
Spell-ing!

What kind of snake is good at math?
An adder!

Which teachers are the most popular?
History teachers. They have lots of dates!

A student's lament: "I have all the right answers. They
    just ask the wrong questions!"

How do little skeletons get to school?
They ride the skull bus!

How is a rabbit like a student who loves math?
They're both good at multiplying!

Why did the rabbit go to barber school?
She wanted to be a harestylist!

Why were the teacher's eyes shining?
Because she had bright pupils!

Spider Dad: "How did you do on your web-spinning test?"
Spider Kid: "Great! I got a bee!"

Where does a train conductor get an education?
At an all aboarding school!

Did you hear about the boy who celebrated whenever he was late for school?
He liked to tardy hardy!

Where did the astronaut get her degree?
At the mooniversity!

Why did the man flunk out of barber school?
He just couldn't cut it!

Why did the school fire the cook?
She was putting too much taste in the food!

What do electricians study in school?
Current events!

Why was the owl a poor student?
He just didn't give a hoot!

What insects always get the best grades?
Bookworms!

Student: "Someday I'd like to teach mathematics."
Counselor: "Then you'll have to get a math-ter's
    degree."

KOOKY KLASSICS

All for pun,

and pun for all!

What's flat and yellow and flies over Never-Never-
 Land?
Peter Pancake!

Why did the Three Little Pigs hire a maid?
Their house was a pigsty!

What do you call a horse who has sat in tar?
Black Booty!

Which of King Arthur's knights was the most fun at a
 party?
Sir Dancelot!

Did you hear the tale of Cinderella the cow?
She had a dairy godmother!

What would you get if you crossed Garfield with Tarzan?
The Lard of the Jungle!

What happened to Rip van Winkle's clothes while he slept?
They got Rip van wrinkled!

Who monkeyed around with the forty thieves?
Ali Baboon!

Who had big ears, a trunk, and a size twenty-seven glass slipper?
Cinderelephant!

Why did Humpty Dumpty have a great fall?
His favorite team won the World Series!

What would you get if you crossed the Roman god of the sea with a bumbler?
Ineptune!

What would you get if you crossed an obnoxious guy
    with a mythical strongman?
Jerkules!

What dog ruled the Knights of the Round Table?
King Arfur!

What has antlers, twelve legs, and swashbuckles?
The Three Mooseketeers!

What famous Dickens novel was about two felines in
    England and France?
A Tale of Two Kitties!

How did Peter Pan help Captain Hook?
He gave him a hand!

What game did Dr. Jekyll like to play?
Hyde and seek!

Who was Tom Sawyer's web-footed friend?
Duck Finn!

Why was Camelot such a fun place to live?
Because of all the knightlife!

Who weighed two hundred pounds and lived with the
    Seven Dwarfs?
Snow Wide!

How did the Seven Dwarfs get home from work so
    quickly?
They took the *short*cut!

What's the difference between Princess Aurora and
    Cinderella?
One's a sleeping beauty and the other's a sweeping
    beauty!

What happened when Cinderella went to the castle?
She had a ball!

How is Pinocchio like Garfield?
They both do a lot of lying around!

What happened when Pinocchio went to Pleasure
  Island?
He nearly made an ass of himself!

What would you get if you crossed Garfield with a famous swordsman?
Zzzzorro!

What would you get if you crossed a fairy tale princess
  with Arlene?
Sleeping Ugly!

Why did Jack climb the beanstalk?
Because it didn't have an elevator!

What would you get if you crossed Odie with a giant?
A big mistake!

How did the Three Bears keep Goldilocks from re-
  entering their house?
They put a Goldi-lock on the door!

What would you get if you crossed Odie with the Big
   Bad Wolf?
A wolf who can drool your house down!

Did you hear about the new sci-fi version of a famous
   bunny tale?
It's called *The Velveteen Robot*!

What would you get if you crossed Garfield with a
   well-known train?
"The Little Engine that Could Eat a Ton!"

What did the old woman say when she returned to the
   shoe?
"There's no lace like home."

Why did the dish run away with the spoon?
Because the knife and fork were too busy cutting up!

What does a naughty genie get for Christmas?
A lamp of coal!

What would you get if you crossed Odie with a famous
    loser of sheep?
Little Bo Pup!

Why was the dragon so sad?
His doctor told him he had to quit smoking!

What would you get if you crossed a fuzzy, yellow bear
    with a virus?
Winnie the Flu!

Why did Cinderella go to the ball in a pumpkin coach?
She couldn't afford a limo!

KNOCK, KNOCK KNONSENSE

Knock, knock!
Who's there?
Mark.
Mark who?
Mark your calendars . . . my birthday's just around the
    corner!

Knock, knock!
Who's there?
Clarence.
Clarence who?
Clarence sale! Everything half price!

Knock, knock!
Who's there?
Aaron.
Aaron who?
Aaron out my stinky gym locker!

Knock, knock!
Who's there?
Stan.
Stan who?
Stan back! Garfield's about to burp!

Knock, knock!
Who's there?
Odie.
Odie who?
Odie food is delicious at de diner!

Knock, knock.
Who's there?
Sid.
Sid who?
Sid down and shuddup!

Knock, knock!
Who's there?
Bea.
Bea who?
Bea cool, fool!

Knock, knock!
Who's there?
Linda.
Linda who?
Linda me a dollar till Friday!

Knock, knock!
Who's there?
Les.
Les who?
Les go crazy!

Knock, knock!
Who's there?
Bjorn.
Bjorn who?
Bjorn to be wild!

Knock, knock.
Who's there?
Annie.
Annie who?
Annie one seen Odie's brain?!

73

Knock, knock!
Who's there?
Hank.
Hank who?
You're welcome!

Knock, knock!
Who's there?
Bess.
Bess who?
Bess get your face outta my space!

Knock, knock!
Who's there?
Jess.
Jess who?
Jess wanted to say "hello!"

Knock, knock!
Who's there?
Ella.
Ella who?
Ella-mentary, my dear doofus!

Knock, knock.
Who's there?
Avery.
Avery who?
Avery-body dance now!

Knock, knock!
Who's there?
Harry.
Harry who?
Harry up ... we're gonna be late for school!

Knock, knock!
Who's there?
Shirley.
Shirley who?
Shirley you'd like to buy some magazines!

Knock, knock!
Who's there?
Don.
Don who?
Don just stand there ... open the door!

Knock, knock!
Who's there?
Bill.
Bill who?
Bill you please stop asking these silly questions?!

Knock, knock!
Who's there?
Walt.
Walt who?
Walt you want, baby, I got!

Knock, knock!
Who's there?
Phil.
Phil who?
Phil like ordering a pizza?

Knock, knock!
Who's there?
Norma Lee.
Norma Lee who?
Norma Lee I don't knock ... I ring the doorbell!

Knock, knock!
Who's there?
Al.
Al who?
Al work and no play is BOR-ING!

Knock, knock!
Who's there?
Justin.
Justin who?
Justin time for dinner, I hope!

Knock, knock!
Who's there?
Cindy.
Cindy who?
Cindy party's over, I might as well go home!

Knock, knock!
Who's there?
Jon.
Jon who?
Jon me in a glass of lemonade?

Knock, knock!
Who's there?
Brett.
Brett who?
Brett you can't guess my last name!

Knock, knock!
Who's there?
Tom.
Tom who?
Tom for another "knock, knock" joke!

Knock, knock!
Who's there?
Barry.
Barry who?
Barry pleased to meet you!

Knock, knock!
Who's there?
Irma.
Irma who?
Irma going to the movies. Wanna come?

Knock, knock!
Who's there?
Hugh.
Hugh who?
Well, yoo-hoo to you, too!

Knock, knock!
Who's there?
Ron.
Ron who?
Ron away before Odie's tongue gets here!

Knock, knock!
Who's there?
Rhoda.
Rhoda who?
Rhoda you a letter. Did you get it?

Knock, knock!
Who's there?
Audrey.
Audrey who?
Audrey enough, *I* don't know either!

Knock, knock!
Who's there?
Arch.
Arch who?
Gesundheit!

Knock, knock!
Who's there?
Mariah.
Mariah who?
Mariah arm is getting tired from all this knocking!

Knock, knock!
Who's there?
Bruce.
Bruce who?
Bruce yourself! You're in for a shock!

Knock, knock!
Who's there?
Brad.
Brad who?
Brad news! Nermal's coming to visit!

Knock, knock!
Who's there?
Evan.
Evan who?
Evan knows what you're doing in there!

Knock, knock!
Who's there?
Carmen.
Carmen who?
Carmen to get you!

Knock, knock!
Who's there?
Chuck.
Chuck who?
Chuck it out! Free pizza!

Knock, knock!
Who's there?
Colleen.
Colleen who?
Colleen up your room, please!

Knock, knock!
Who's there?
Dennis.
Dennis who?
Dennis players make a lot of racquet!

Knock, knock!
Who's there?
Mike.
Mike who?
Mike me a sandwich, will you?

Knock, knock!
Who's there?
Candice.
Candice who?
Candice be the last "knock, knock" joke?

What would you get if you cloned Nermal?
Double trouble!

What does Garfield call a slobbering dog?
A drool fool!

What do you call a so-so comedian?
A mediocre joker!

What has four legs, antlers, and has escaped from the
    zoo?
A loose moose!

What do you call a grizzly who's just won the lottery?
A millionaire bear!

What do you call a rodent who runs in front of a bus?
A splat rat!

What do you call a parrot who never stops talking?
A wordy birdy!

What did the zookeeper use to clean up after the elephants?
A super duper pooper scooper!

What do you call a toddler who's a movie star?
A hotshot tot!

What would you get if you crossed Odie with the god of love?
A stupid Cupid!

What do you call a deer who's a wimp?
A namby-pamby Bambi!

What do you call an overweight feline?
A flabby tabby!

What does Garfield call a sudden urge to eat?
A snack attack!

What do you call a pig with a pocket protector?
A dorky porky!

What do you call a taxi driver who doesn't get tipped?
A crabby cabby!

Why did the rodents help the old lady across the
street?
They were nice mice!

What do you call the head of a cattle rustling gang?
The chief beef thief!

What do fast runners have?
Fleet feet!

What do you call a spring flower who does magic
tricks?
A hocus pocus crocus!

What quacks and has a four-leaf clover?
A lucky ducky!

What do you call a humongous dinosaur bone?
A colossal fossil!

What do you call a tiny cat?
An itty-bitty kitty!

What do you call electricity made from lemons?
Sour power!

What do you call a cowardly monkey?
A wimp chimp!

What do you call a meeting of dogs?
A bowwow powwow!

What do you call a basketball star in prison?
A slammer jammer!

What happened when Jon tried to fix the ceiling?
A plaster disaster!

What do you call a sad "king of the beasts"?
A cryin' lion!

What do you call a crabby New York baseball player?
A cranky Yankee!

What do you call Jon's smelly aftershave lotion?
Geek reek!

Why did the man jab the frog with his finger?
He was a croaker poker!

What did Jon's neighbor say when Garfield ate her
    flowers?
"Drat that fat cat!"

How does a Scotsman cook his dinner?
In a Scot pot!

What is it that makes people seasick?
Ocean motion!

Why did Garfield march into the bakery?
He was on roll patrol!

Did you hear about the oyster who wanted to get away
from the world?
He went to an oyster cloister!

What do you call a party at the garbage dump?
A trash bash!

What do you call a butcher who throws his cutting
instruments?
A cleaver heaver!

Did you hear about the poor farmer who was always
smiling?
He was a pleasant peasant!

Does Odie have enough sense to come in out of the
    rain?
No, he's often a soggy doggy!

Did you hear about the delicious dip that's made by
    monks?
It's called "Holy Guacamole!"

What do you call a phony physician?
A mock doc!

Does Garfield like people who like to work out?
No, he's an exerciser despiser!

What does Jon hear when Odie wants to come inside?
A canine whine!

What happened when Nermal fell in love?
He was a smitten kitten!

What did the Cyclops say to his girlfriend?
"I only have eye for you!"

How much does Garfield love Pooky?
Beary much!

Why did the pig give his girlfriend a box of candy?
It was Valenswine's Day!

"I think Amy and Steve make a pretty weird couple."
"Yeah, she's pretty and he's weird!"

What did the farmer give his wife for Valentine's Day?
A hog and a kiss!

What did the lizard say to his girlfriend?
"Iguana love you forever!"

Did you hear about the marathon runners who fell in
love?
They had a long-distance romance!

What did the boy firefly say to the girl firefly?
"I really glow for you!"

What sound do porcupines make when they kiss?
"Ouch! Ouch! Ouch! Oooo! Ouch!"

What do you call it when dogs kiss?
A pooch smooch!

Why did the lobster break up with her boyfriend?
He was a crab!

Knock, Knock!
Who's there?
Mary.
Mary who?
Mary me and we'll live happily ever after!

96

What happened when the boy gorilla was dumped by his girlfriend?
He went ape!

Knock, knock!
Who's there?
Darwin.
Darwin who?
Darwin, I weally wuv you!

Did you hear about the romance in the tropical fish tank?
It was a case of guppy love.

Why wouldn't the cow go out with the bull?
She wasn't in the moo-d!

What happened when the snowman tried to kiss his date?
He got the cold shoulder!

Arlene: "If a woman married Jon, what would you give her?"
Garfield: "My condolences!"

Where is Garfield's favorite place to look for love?
In the mirror!

What happened when the vampire met the beautiful woman?
It was love at first bite!

Does Garfield really love high-calorie desserts?
Oh, yes. He's completely in*fat*uated!

What would you call a woman who goes out with Jon?
Scarred for life!

What do you call two birds in love?
Tweethearts!

What did the painter say to his girlfriend?
"I love you with all my art!"

What would you call it if your wedding day was December 25th?
A Marry Christmas!

Did you hear about the pigeon couple?
They were very lovey-dovey.

What happened when Jon took his date to the dog
    show?
She won!

How can you show a Dutch girl that you love her?
Kiss her on her tulips!

What do snake couples do after they have a fight?
They hiss and make up!

Why can't Garfield ever marry Arlene?
Because he's already engaged to himself!

What would you call a romance in a famous French
    museum?
A Louvre affair!

What's a dog's idea of a romantic gesture?
Drinking champagne out of the toilet!

Did you hear about the lawyer with a broken heart?
Of course not. A lawyer doesn't *have* a heart!

What did the boy pig say to the girl pig?
"I wanna hold your ham!"

Knock, Knock!
Who's there?
Lena.
Lena who?
Lena little closer and gimme a kiss!

What did the girl angel say to the boy angel?
"I love you with all my harp!"

What's the difference between Jon and a hermit?
A hermit has more dates.

What happened when the two volcanoes met?
It was lava at first sight!

Why did the gorilla give bananas to his girlfriend?
Because he loved her a bunch!

What did one computer say to the other?
"You've got a nice interface."

Nermal: "Did Jon ever have a steady girlfriend?"
Garfield: "He did once."
Nermal: "What happened?"
Garfield: "The zoo finally tracked her down."

Arlene: "Garfield, could I interest you in a dinner for
    two?"
Garfield: "Sure, but what are *you* going to eat?"

Jon was hoping to date some classier women this year,
    but all the bag ladies turned him down!

What frontier lawman was famous for his indigestion?
Wyatt Burp!

What would you get if you crossed Garfield with an
    Egyptian queen?
Cleofatra!

What was sweet, yellow, and got creamed by Sitting
    Bull?
George Armstrong Custard!

What famous Mongol conqueror was sent to prison?
Genghis Convict!

Who was the first European dog to explore the Orient?
Barco Polo!

Why did George Washington chop down the cherry
   tree with his hatchet?
His mom wouldn't let him use the chain saw.

Teacher: "What caused the fall of Rome?"
Student: "I think it slipped on Greece."

Teacher: "Where is Plymouth Rock?"
Student: "Right next to Plymouth Bush."

What would you get if you crossed a famous frontiers-
   man with a pickle?
Buffalo Dill!

Teacher: "Who was the handsomest man in English
   history?"
Student: "King Henry the Eighth. He was always making women lose their heads!"

What would you get if you crossed a cookie with the
   discoverer of the law of gravity?
Sir Isaac Fig Newton!

What was Ivan the Terrible's favorite kiddie song?
"Twinkle, twinkle, little czar!"

What would you get if you crossed one of the Founding Fathers with a famous monster?
Benjamin Franklinstein!

What barbarian conqueror was also a male model?
Attila the Hunk!

What's round, purple, and almost conquered the world?
Alexander the Grape!

What would you get if you crossed a famous Confederate general with a pesky insect?
Robert E. Flea!

How is putting Garfield on a diet like the 1929 stock market crash?
They both lead to a great depression!

Where did Native Americans buy their tomahawks?
At the chopping mall!

In the Middle Ages, what did most people get for
    Christmas?
The plague!

What was General Grant's favorite tree?
The infantry!

Who is Odie's favorite U.S. president?
Rover Cleveland!

What would you get if you crossed a vegetable with
    the first president of the United States?
George Squashington!

What would you get if you crossed the inventor of the
    telephone with a cinnamon snack?
Alexander Graham Cracker!

Why did Paul Revere yell "The Martians are coming!"?
His horse had just kicked him in the head!

What would you get if you crossed Garfield with Eric
    the Red?
A Viking who only raids the refrigerator!

108

What's the difference between Queen Isabella's husband and Jon Arbuckle?
One's a Ferd and the other's a nerd!

What happened when King Tut misbehaved?
His parents sent him to his tomb!

What had long legs, wore a coonskin cap, and got squished at the Alamo?
Davy Cricket!

What kind of gun did a dumb cowboy use?
A Dolt .45!

Who is known as the "Father of Phony Psychiatry"?
Sigmund Fraud!

What famous words were spoken by the first pig to set foot on the moon?
"That's one small step for a ham. One giant leap for hamkind!"

What famous Roman general was known for his terrible colds?
Julius Sneezer!

What potbellied explorer searched for the "Fountain of Youth"?
Paunch de Leon!

Who is Garfield's favorite military genius?
Nap-oleon!

Teacher: "How did the first explorers get to America?"
Student: "On a bus."
Teacher: "A bus?"
Student: "Yeah. A Colum-bus!"

Why did Abraham Lincoln grow a beard?
He wanted to look like that guy on the five-dollar bill.

What's the difference between Teddy Roosevelt and Odie?
One carried a big stick and the other carries a big lick!

Who had a beard, webbed feet, and wrote *A Christmas Carol*?
Charles Duckens!

What would you get if you crossed a Kentucky
   explorer with a dried fruit?
Daniel Prune!

What did George Washington say to his army at Valley
   Forge?
"Sorry, men. The flights to Florida are all booked up!"

Teacher: "What did Napoleon say about his defeat at
   Waterloo?"
Student: "Something in French, I'll bet!"

What would you get if you crossed a buccaneer with a
   hairstylist?
A Barber-y pirate!

Why did the Pilgrims have the first Thanksgiving?
They wanted another excuse to watch football.

daffy
definitions

alarm clock: A device for waking people who don't have kids or pets.

Arbuckle: From the Latin *arbuculus*, "wiener-chested"; a geek; a nerd; a geeky nerd; you get the picture.

bed: Furniture piece designed for that most exciting of all activities—sleep.

bird: A feathered flying cat snack.

brother: A common household pest; synonymous with "bother."

calories: The best-tasting bits of any food. Take thousands, they're small.

car: An automotive machine that almost any doofus is allowed to operate; but can a cat get a license? Noooooooo!

cat: A highly intelligent and attractive animal of the feline persuasion; nature's most perfect pet.

chocolate: A sweet, highly fattening substance; one of the four basic food groups.

Christmas: December holiday that promotes the spirit of getting; also has some religious significance.

claw: A cat's best friend; a drape's worst nightmare.

diet: Like "die" with a "t"; an eating program that removes excess pounds and your will to live.

dog: A brainless, four-legged flea magnet whose breath could stun a moose.

dream: A fantasy, like no-cal lasagna, or a woman who thinks Jon is cool.

eat: What one does between naps.

exercise: Any completely unnecessary physical activity, such as jogging or rolling over.

fat: Overweight; obese; Santa-waisted; in other words, just right.

french fries: Slivers of potato cooked in hot oil; best when eaten or stuck in your nose.

Halloween: Ancient Celtic celebration of the dead that has evolved quite nicely into an excuse to eat candy until you explode.

homework: Cruel and unusual punishment best suffered in front of the TV.

kitten: A small, cuddly animal used to trick people into buying cats.

lasagne: Nature's most perfect food.

lazy: Indolent, slothful; in extreme cases, comatose.

mailman: One who delivers the mail; see also scratching post.

mouse: Furry, germ-infested, cheese-licking rodent. This is suitable cat cuisine? I don't think so.

morning: The bad end to a good night; would be much better if it started later.

Nermal: The world's cutest kitten; soon to become extinct.

Odie: A type of dog or fungus; it's hard to tell.

parent: An adult keeper of children; not easily understood, but at least they provide snacks and TV.

party: A type of fun assembly guaranteed by the Constitution; see also soiree, wing-ding, riot.

pet: A domestic animal who provides love and companionship in exchange for blind obedience and twelve square meals a day.

pizza: Delicious tomato and cheese plant which scientists have trained to grow in flat, cardboard boxes. It's true!

Pooky: A huggable "beddy" bear who never says a harsh word . . . or anything else.

school: An educational institution designed to train your brain, assuming they can find it.

sister: An annoying female sibling usually found in the bathroom.

sleep: A state of unconsciousness best experienced in large quantities; also the perfect exercise.

snoring: The loud, irritating breathing of a sleeper; easily remedied with a pair of cymbals.

spider: Web-spinning, eight-legged insect; generally harmless, especially if bludgeoned with a sledgehammer.

teacher: One who instructs; comes in "good," "bad," and "ogre" models.

telephone: A communication device permanently attached to an adolescent's ear.

television: Device that receives mind-numbing video signals; don't grow up without it.

tomorrow: The best time for starting anything unpleasant, like homework or a diet.

veterinarian: A doctor who treats animals, whether they like it or not; synonymous with "needles as long as your arm."

JOKING LIKE CATS AND DOGS

What do you call a cat who's a lawyer?
An attorney at claw!

What kind of food do upscale dogs eat?
Yuppie Chow!

What do you call a kitty who looks through keyholes?
A peeping tomcat!

What would you get if you crossed "The Terminator"
    with a cat?
A dog's worst nightmare!

Why did the dog run away from home?
He wanted a new leash on life!

Why did all the people wipe their feet on the dog?
Because he was a doormutt!

What kind of dog works at the United Nations?
A diplomutt!

How do space cats drink their milk?
From flying saucers!

Why did Odie rap the side of his head against the
 piano keys?
He was playing by ear!

Why should dogs wear collars?
It makes them easier to hang up.

What do you call a cat who sleeps eighteen hours a
 day?
An insomniac.

Will a cat come if he's called?
Yes, but he prefers a written invitation.

If you decide to train your cat, what should you do first?
Forget the whole idea!

What's the easiest way to get a cat out of a tree?
Send up a pit bull.

What do you call a dog who digs up ancient bones?
A barkeologist!

Why was the movie director filming a dog?
He was making a dogumentary!

What do you call a fear of being scratched by a cat?
Clawstrophobia!

What did the cat say to the mean dog?
"I'll be fleeing you!"

"I think my dog is really stupid."
"Why do you think that?"
"He's a dog!"

Why did the cat hiss at the Republican?
She was a Democat!

Where does a cat keep his claws?
In the clawset!

What kind of dog perspires the most?
An Irish sweater!

How can you tell a male cat from a female cat?
The male cat always leaves the seat up on the
    litterbox.

What do you call a dog whose offspring have off-
    spring?
Grandpaw!

What would you get if you crossed a cat with a floor
    covering?
A Purrsian rug!

Why wouldn't they let the foreign cat into this coun-
    try?
He didn't have a pussport!

Dog 1: "All the dogs in the neighborhood seem to like you."
Dog 2: "Oh, yes. I'm very pupular!"

What do you call a criminal who steals cats?
A purr snatcher!

How did the cat catch the mouse?
He hid in the cupboard and made a noise like a cheese.

What would you get if you crossed a cat with a Cuban dictator?
Fidel Cat-stro!

What did the dog say to his tail?
"I wish you'd stop following me!"

According to Garfield, what always looks good on a dog?
Tire tracks!

"I've got good news and bad news about your dog," said the vet. "The bad news is your dog only has half a brain."

"What's the good news, Doctor?"

"You've got the smartest dog in the world!"

Do cats sweat?
No, but they do purrspire!

What kind of dog is always snoozing on the job?
An English sleepdog!

How do you know when your cat is too lazy?
You have to dust him twice a week.

"I just had my cat's claws removed."
"So why are *you* limping?"
"I had them removed from my leg."

Did you hear about the dog who backed into the electric outlet?
It's a shocking tail!

"Have you had your cat fixed?"
"I didn't even know he was broken!"

What did the cat say as he ate the plant?
"Hey, what are fronds for?"

Customer: "I'm returning this cat food."
Clerk: "What's the problem?"
Customer: "It says it comes in an 'easy opening can.' "
Clerk: "So?"
Customer: "My cat tried for three days, and he never
    could open it!"

What would you get if you crossed a dog with Arnold
    Schwarzenegger?
A dog who can fetch your refrigerator!

Why did the candidate go the the dentist?
It was time for his 50,000 smile checkup!

What's red and white and blue all over?
A candy cane holding its breath!

What do you call the hair above a mouse's upper lip?
A mouse-tache!

What did the envelope say to the stamp?
"Stick with me and you'll go far!"

Where do cows like to go for fun?
To an a-moos-ment park!

What would you call a land where Odie was king?
A kingdumb!

Life is a party. And Jon's invitation got lost in the mail!

Did you hear about the rich old man whose possible
heirs were dying off?
He had a receding heir-line!

How does a schizophrenic change a light bulb?
He asks one of his personalities to do it for him!

What do you call a fear of being trapped in a chimney
with a fat man?
Santa Claustrophobia!

What would you get if you crossed a hog with a
mouse?
A little pig-squeak!

What would you get if you crossed a hippo with a rabbit?
A hoppopotamus!

What would you call a dinosaur who's a lousy driver?
Tyrannosaurus Wrecks!

What kinds of music does a leprechaun band play?
Shamrock 'n' roll!

Did you hear about the train engine that went crazy?
It was a loco-motive!

What's black and white and green all over?
A seasick penguin!

What has ears, but can't hear?
A cornfield!

What's black and white and blue all over?
A depressed zebra!

What type of shoes are most like Garfield?
Loafers!

Why wasn't the astronaut in her office?
She was out to launch!

If a human baby gets a birth certificate, what did baby
    Garfield get?
A girth certificate!

What game does Garfield like to play with Odie?
Tongue-of-war!

What animals make the worst entertainers?
Skunks. Their acts always stink!

What has flippers, a tail, and warns about the dangers
    of smoking?
The Sturgeon General!

How does a lawyer change a light bulb?
He doesn't. He just sues the light bulb company!

What do you call a porcupine wearing a tuxedo?
A sharp dresser!

Knock, Knock!
Who's there?
Hoo.
Hoo who?
Hey, is there an owl in there?

Why did they call the exterminator to the county court
    house?
The place was infested with lawyers!

"John, use the word 'contrive' in a sentence."
"As soon as I get my license, then I contrive."

"Jean, use the word 'awful' in a sentence."
"Awful out of the tree and broke my leg."

"Jenny, use the word 'cinder' in a sentence."
"When the girl got sick at school, the teacher had to
    cinder home."

"Jason, use the word 'doctrine' in a sentence."
"That sick girl could use some doctrine."

"Jill, use the word 'terrify' in a sentence."
"I don't terrify go to the dance or not."

"Joey, use the word 'torrid' in a sentence."
"I torrid a big hole in my new shirt."

"Jessica, use the word 'stark' in a sentence."
"When you turn out all the lights, it's stark."

"Jeremy, use the word 'despair' in a sentence."
"Do you like despair of shoes or the other one?"

"Joan, use the word 'alibi' in a sentence."
"Alibi a new pen when this one runs out."

"Jemma, use the word 'ally' in a sentence."
"Ally want to do is sleep, sleep, sleep."

"Jordan, use the word 'pressure' in a sentence."
"You should never pressure head with a waffle iron."

"Joyce, use the word 'hence' in a sentence."
"The farmer had one rooster and six hence."

"Jacob, use the word 'vain' in a sentence."
"Vain it starts to rain, I go inside."

"JoBeth, use the word 'menu' in a sentence."
"I'll try not to get dirt on menu dress."

"Janine, use the word 'aghast' in a sentence."
"My dad buys his gas at aghast station."

"Jody, use the word 'bigotry' in a sentence."
"A California redwood is a very bigotry."

"Joshua, use the word 'harmony' in a sentence."
"Harmony puns like these can a person stand?"

STRIPS, SPECIALS, OR BESTSELLING BOOKS...
GARFIELD'S ON EVERYONE'S MENU
Don't miss even one episode in the Tubby Tabby's hilarious series!